2 two

GW01551602

① ⑦
LIN ¦ ICA

② ⑧
TOM ¦ ERT

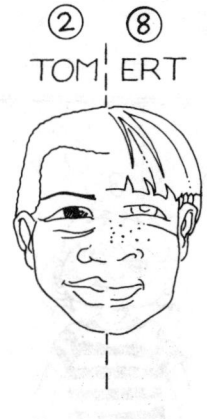

⑨AL¦MY

④ ⑩
MON ¦ LY

⑤ ⑪
MAR ¦ DA

⑥ ⑫
ROB ¦ TIN

Let's talk

What's the name of number four?
　　I think it's Monica.

What's the name of number . . . .?
　■ I think it's . . . .
　■ I don't know yet.

Let's write

1　The name of number one is..

2　The name of number two is..

3　The name of number three is..

4　The name of number four is..

5　The name of number five is..

6　The name of number six is..

3 three

Let's talk

Are you number eleven?
    Yes, I am.

Are you number . . .?
- ■ Yes, I am.
- ■ No, I'm not.

4 four

a cow

a tiger

a horse

a cat

a lion

a bird

an elephant

a dog

1 2 3 4 5 6 7 8

Let's talk

What's this?
    I think it's a lion.

What's this?
- I think it's a . . . .
- I don't know.
- What's . . . in English?

Let's write

1   Number one is a...

2   Number two is a...

3   Number three...

4   Number four...

5   ....

6   ....

7   ....

8   ....

5 five

Let's talk

I'm thinking of an animal.
It's big.
     Is it number one?
Yes, it is.

I'm thinking of an animal.

It's
■ big.
■ small.
■ not a . . . .
■ not an . . . .

     Is it number . . .?
■ Yes, it is.
■ No, it isn't.

Let's write

1   Number one is a d..   It's b..

2   Number two is an..   It's..

3   Number three is a..   It's..

4   Number four is a..   It's..

5   Number five..   ....   It's..

6   Number six..   ....   It's..

6 six

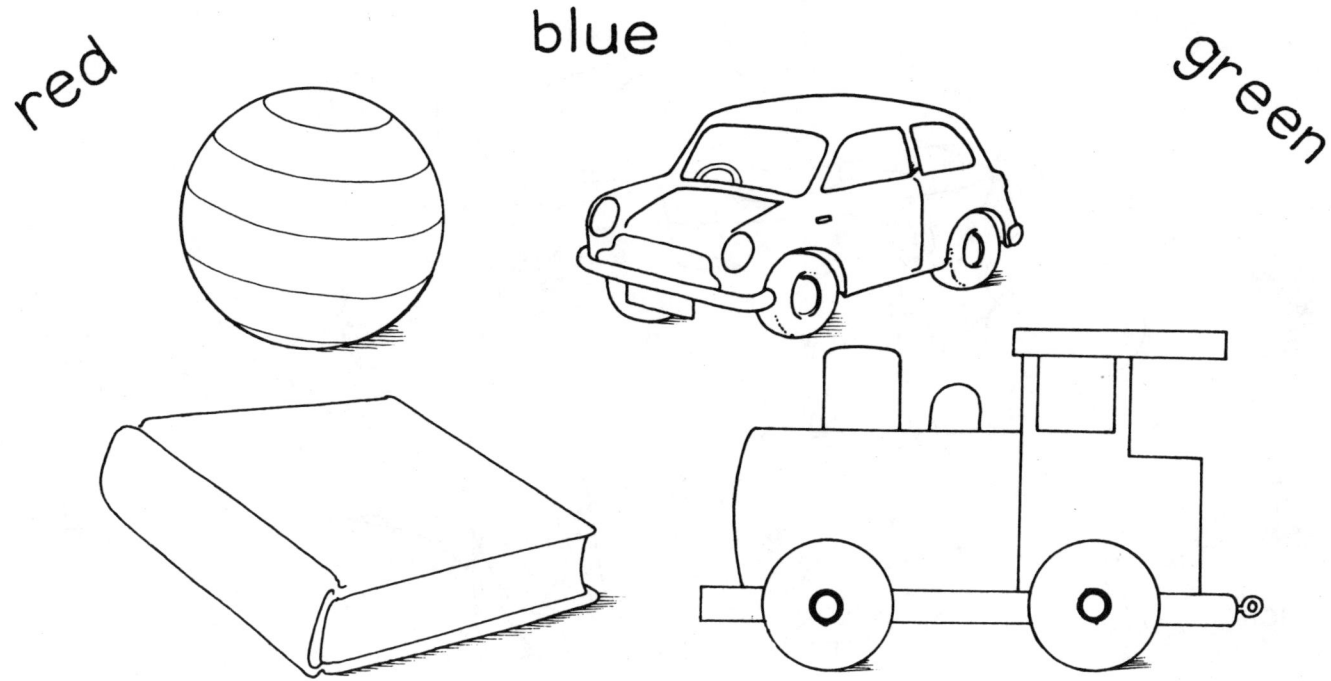

red
blue
green

Let's talk

I've got a red ball. What have you got?

I've got a green ball.

I've got a ■ red
■ green . . . . What have you got?
■ blue

I've got a ■ red
■ green . . . .
■ blue

I've got a ■ red
■ green . . . ., too.
■ blue

Let's write

1   I have got a..ball.

2   I..a..book.

3   I..a..train.

Let's talk

What's Nick got?

I think he's got a big dog.

What's . . . got?

■ I think
  ■ he's
  ■ she's got a . . . .

■ I don't know yet.

Let's write

1   Emma has got a...

2   Peter has got a...

3   Nick has...

4   Janet...

5   Bob...

6   Lucy..

Let's talk

Who's fat and has got a long nose?

John is fat and has got a long nose.

Who's . . . and has got a . . .?

■ Is it . . .?

■ . . . is . . . and has got a . . . .

Let's write

1 ....is fat and has got a long nose.

2 ....is fat and has got a big hat.

3 ....is thin and................ ....a big hat.

4 ....is thin and................ ....a long nose.

5 ....is t........and................ ....a small hat.

6 ....is f........and................ ....a small mouth.

7 ....is f........and................ ....a big mouth.

8 ....is f........and................ ....a short nose.

9 nine

planes   balls   horses   cow   ships   cars   train

DICK   SANDRA   DAVID

MIKE   SUE   PAMELA

Let's talk

What toys has Sue got?
> I don't know. Just a minute.

What toys has . . . got?
> ■ I don't know. Just a minute.

> ■ He's   ■ a
>   got   . . . .
> ■ She's   ■ some

Let's write

1   Dick has got some........................ and some........................

2   Sandra........................ a........................ and some........................

3   David........................ some........................ and some........................

4   Mike........................ a........................ and some........................

5   Sue........................ some........................ and some........................

6   Pamela........................ a........................ and some........................

10 ten

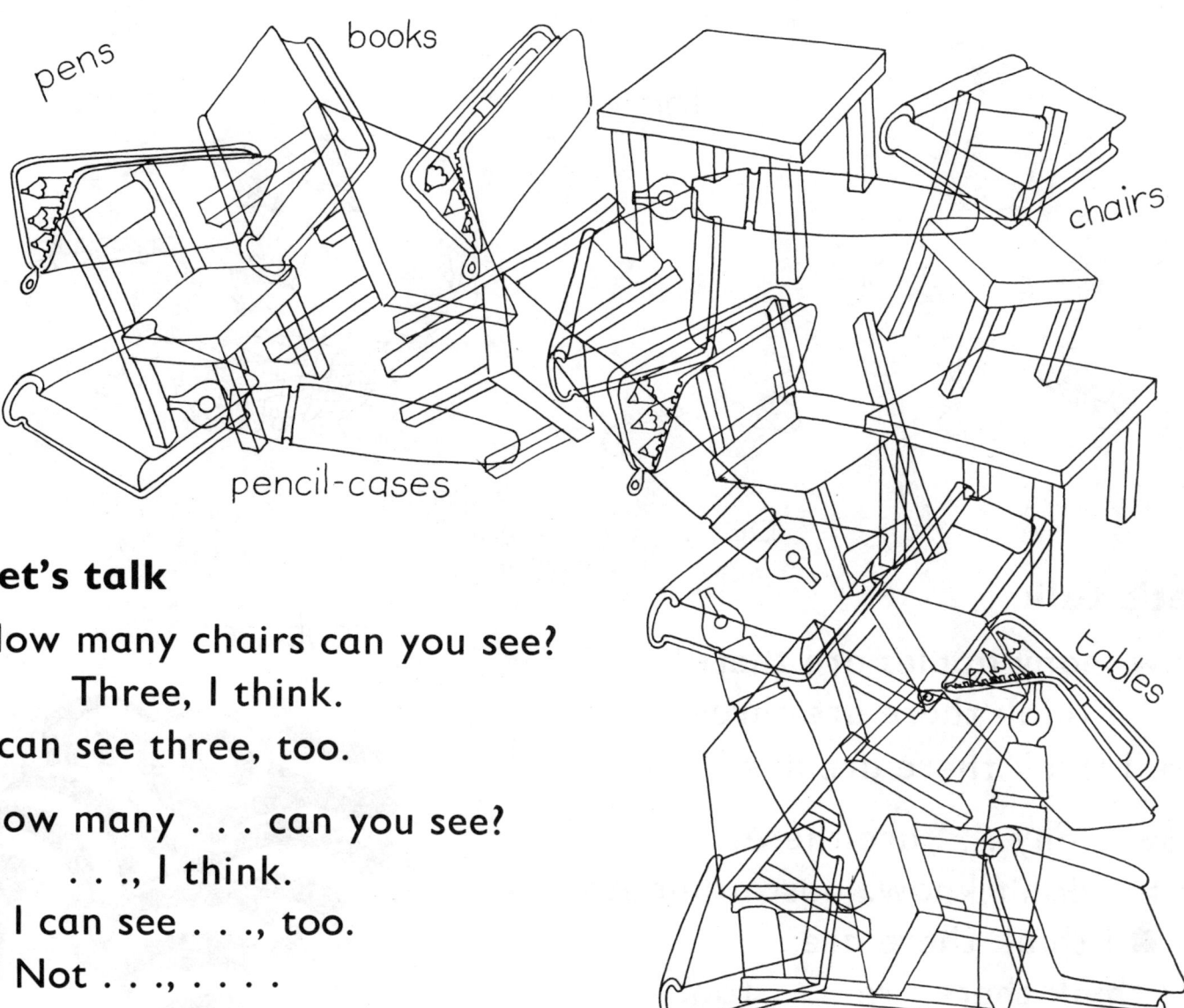

pens

books

chairs

pencil-cases

tables

Let's talk

How many chairs can you see?
        Three, I think.
I can see three, too.

How many . . . can you see?
        . . ., I think.
■ I can see . . ., too.
■ Not . . ., ...

Let's write

1   How many tables can you see?

       I can see........................tables.

2   How many pencil-cases can you see?

       I can........................   ....pencil-cases.

3   How many books can you see?

       I........................books.

4   ....pens can you see?

       I........................pens.

5   ....chairs can you see?

       I........................chairs.

apples

long

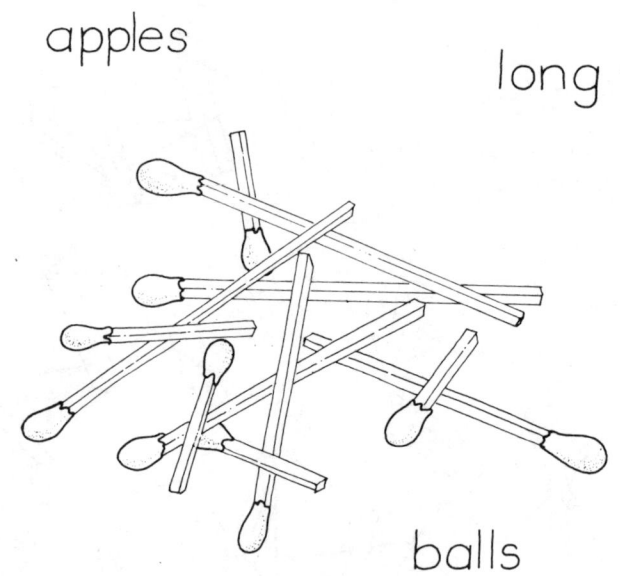

balls

short

small   big

Let's talk

How many apples are there?
    I think there are three.
No, I think there are five.

How many . . . are there?
    ■ I don't know. Just a minute.
    ■ I think there are . . . .
■ I think there are . . ., too.
■ No, I think there are . . . .

matches

Let's write

1   There are................................matches.

2   There are................................long m............................

3   There are................................short m...........................

4   There..apples.

5   ....big a...................................

6   ....small a.................................

7   ....balls.

8   ....b..................b......................

9   ....sm.................b......................

12 twelve

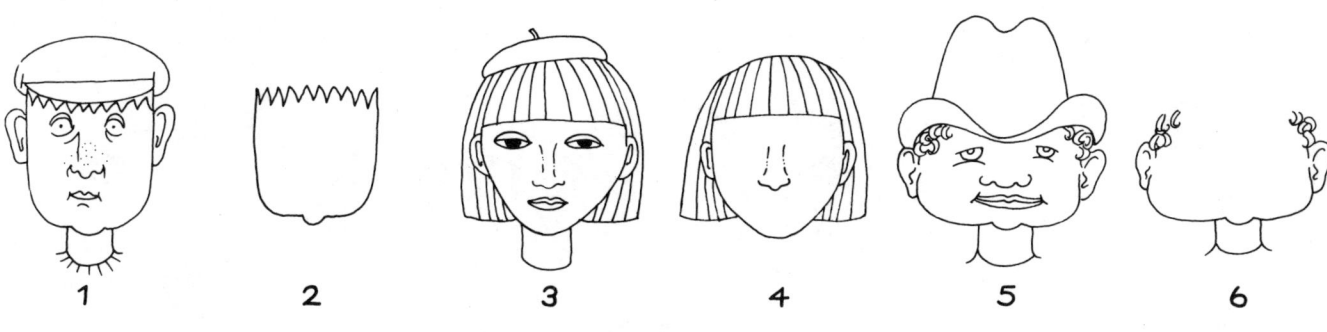

1 2 3 4 5 6

face

nose

ears

an eye   mouth   an ear

hair

neck   eyes

Let's talk

Number two has got no ears.
Draw two ears!

Number . . . has got no . . . .
Draw . . . . . .!

Let's write

an e............   h............   an e............

two ....s   a n............   two e....s

a n............   a m............   a h............   a f............

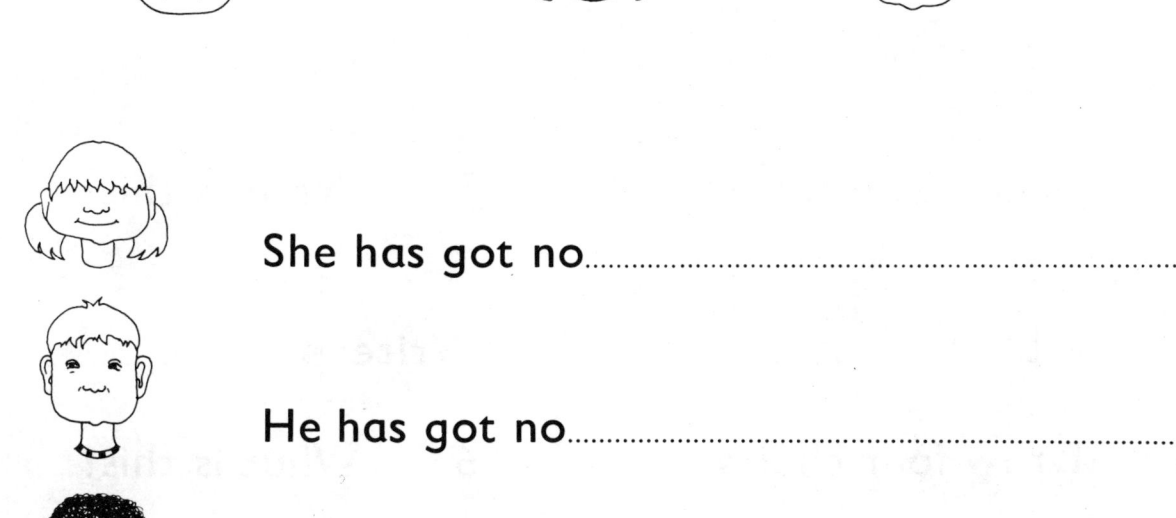

She has got no..

He has got no..

He has.. no..

13 thirteen

Let's talk

Which animal can we draw tail E on?
　　　　Draw it on the cow.
No, that's wrong.　Draw it on the dog.

Which animal can we draw tail . . . on?
　　　　Draw it on the . . . .
■ That's right.
■ No, that's wrong.　Draw it on the . . . .

Let's draw and write

1　　Draw two hats:

4　　Draw a small boy:

2　　What is this?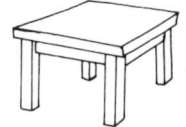

Write: t........................

5　　What is this?

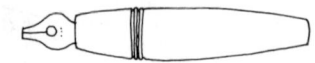

Write: p........................

3　　Draw four chairs:

6　　What is this?

Write: c........................

Which animals can you see?
Write them here.

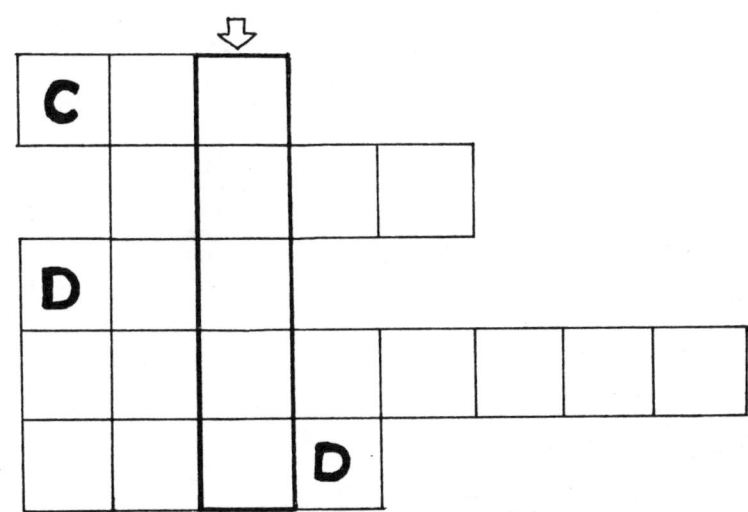

Let's draw

'Give me my hat, please'.

Give the boy his ears.

Give the girl a nose.

14 fourteen

Let's talk

Where's A?

    I think A is on the ear.

No, I think A is on the mouth.

Where's . . .?

    I think . . . is . . . .

■ I think so, too.

■ No, I think . . . is . . . .

Let's write

1   A is..

2   B is..

3   C is..

4   D is..

5   E is..

6   F is..

7   G is..

15 fifteen

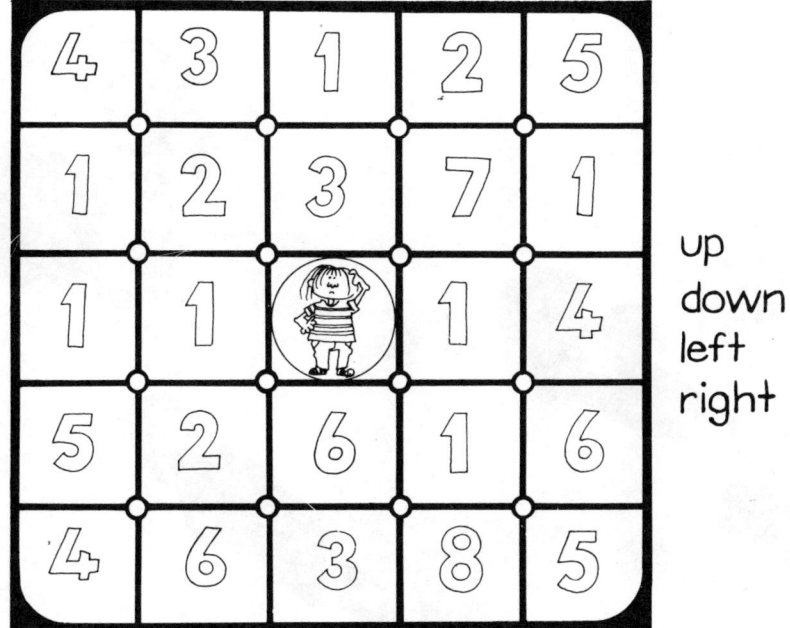

up
down
left
right

Let's talk

Can you help me, please?
    Go up.
That's three. Can you help me, please?

Can you help me, please?
    Go . . . .
That's . . . . Can you help me, please?

Let's write

Can you make twelve?

1   three + seven + one + one = twelve

2   six + ... = twelve

3   one + ... = twelve

4   one + ... = twelve

5   seven + ... = twelve

6   one + ... = twelve

7   two + ... = twelve

8   two + ... = twelve

16 sixteen

Let's talk

Is D Mary's shadow?

    Yes, I think so.

Is D Peter's shadow?

    No, I don't think so. It's Mary's shadow.

Is . . . . . .'s shadow?

  ■ Yes, I think so.

  ■ No, I don't think so. It's . . .'s shadow.

Let's write

1   A is................................'s shadow.

2   B is................................'s shadow.

3   C is................................'s shadow.

4   D is................................'s shadow.

5   E..

6   F..

7   G..

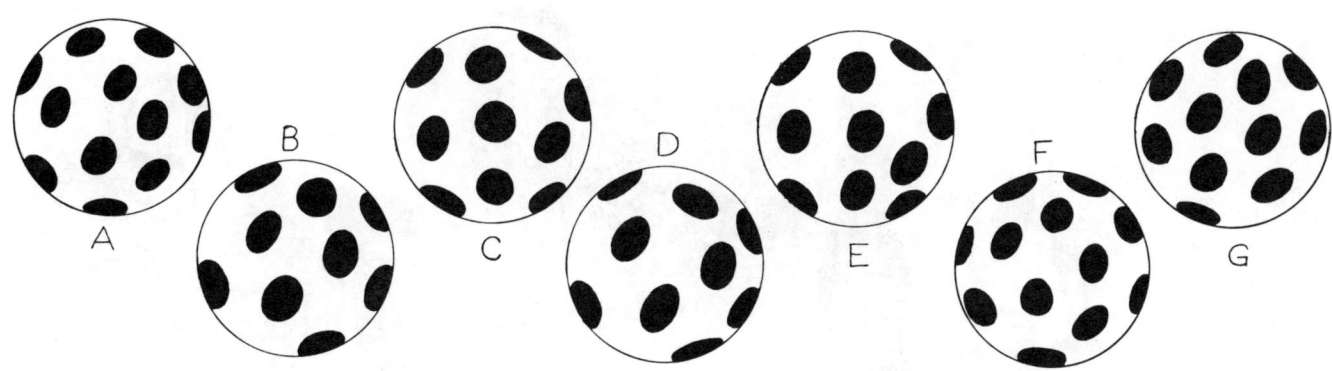

Let's talk

Look at ball A and ball B. Are they the same?
   No, they aren't. A has twelve spots and B has nine spots.

Look at ball . . . and ball . . . . Are they the same?
  ■ Yes, they are.
  ■ No, they aren't. . . . has . . . spots and . . . has . . . spots.

Let's write: Yes, they are or No, they aren't

1   Look at ball F and ball D. Are they the same?

   ....

2   Look at B and C. Are they the same?

   ....

3   Look at C and E. Are they the same?

   ....

4   Look at D and G. Are they the same?

   ....

5   Look at A and F. Are they the same?

   ....

6   Look at B and D. Are they the same?

   ....

18 eighteen

MIKE AND JIM DON AND JANE ANN AND SAM SUSAN AND DAVID TED AND MOLLY MARY AND DIANA

 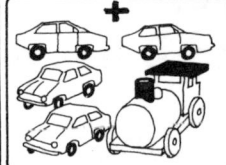    

Let's talk

What have Susan and David got?
  They've got three ships and one plane.

What have . . . and . . . got?
  ■ I don't know yet.
  ■ They've got . . . .

Let's write

1   *Sam and Ann:* They have got ....

2   *Don and Jane:* They ....

3   *Susan and David:* They ....

4   *Mary and Diana:* ....

5   *Ted and Molly:* ....

6   *Mike and Jim:* ....

19 nineteen

Let's talk

Look at doll A.   What's missing?
     She hasn't got a right arm.

a) Look at doll . . . .   What's missing?
- She hasn't got . . . .
- I don't know yet.
- Just a minute.

b) Look at . . . and . . . .   What's missing?
     They haven't got . . . .

Let's write

1   A hasn't got..

2   B hasn't got..

3   C..

4   D..

5   C and E haven't got...

6   A and B.....................got...

7   A and D..

8   E and F..

20 twenty

Let's talk

Whose ball is number eleven?

     I think it's the football player's. And you, Peter?

I think so, too.

Whose . . . is number . . .?

     I think it's the . . .'s. And you, . . .?

■ I think so, too.

■ I think it's the . . .'s.

Let's write

1   Number one is the...................'s ....

2   Number two is the...................'s ....

3   Number th........................... is the...................'s ....

4   Number f............................. is the...................'s ....

5   Number............................... is the...

6   N.. is the...............................

7   N...

8   ....

9   ....

10 ....

ANN DAVID

Let's talk

Has Ann got the right hat?
>   No, I think she's got David's.

Has
- Ann
- David
got the right . . .?

- No, I think
  - he's
  - she's
  got . . .'s.

- Yes, I think so.
- I don't know.

Let's write

1   Ann has got David's...

2   David has got Ann's...

3   Ann has got...

4   David has...

5   Ann...

6   David...

Let's talk

Write . . .!

Let's write

How many words?

....

....

23 twenty-three

COLOUR THIS PAGE

b = blue
y = yellow
r = red
w = white
g = green

short
big
round
long
square
small

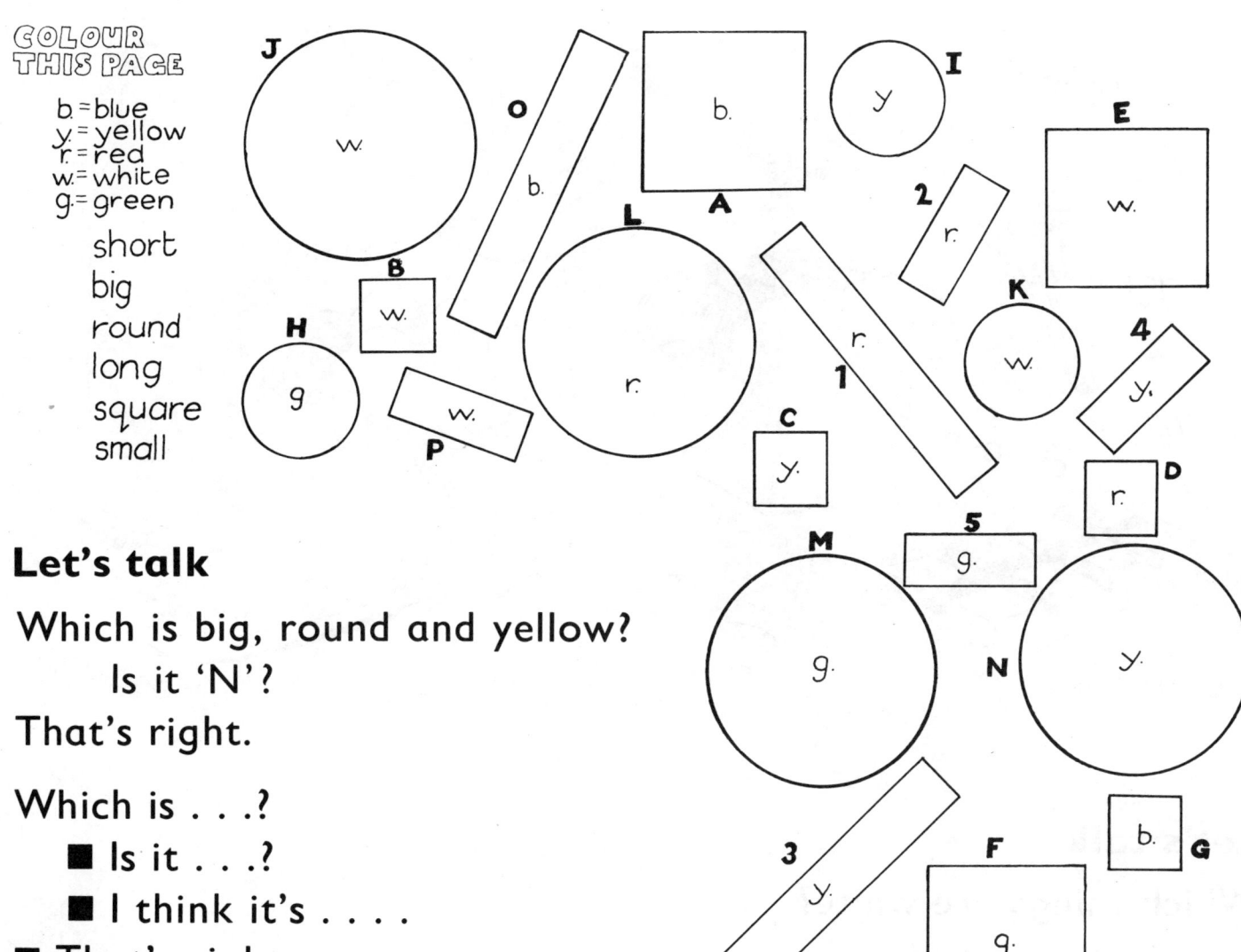

Let's talk

Which is big, round and yellow?

　　　Is it 'N'?

That's right.

Which is . . . .?

- ■ Is it . . . .?
- ■ I think it's . . . .
- ■ That's right.
- ■ No.

Let's write

1　　A is big, square and blue.

2　　B is ...., ... and ....

3　　J is ...., ... and ....

4　　K is ...., ... and ....

5　　O is l........................ .... and b.................................

6　　P is .... and ....

7　　Which is long and yellow? ....

8　　Which is big, round and green? ....

9　　Which is small, square and white? ....

Let's talk

Which things are white?

    Milk, . . . and . . . .

Which things are . . .?

    . . ., . . . and . . . .

Let's write

1   Butter is y...

2   Bread is b...

3   Ice-cream..............w...............................

4   Bananas are y...

5   Eggs are w...

6   I..................., e.........s and m.......... are w.........................

7   B............, b............ and c............ are y.........................

8   T............, b............ and c.........................

blue   red   orange

grey   green

Let's talk

What colour ■ is an orange?
■ are trees?
■ can flowers be?

What colour ■ is . . .?
■ are . . .?
■ can . . . be?

■ It   ■ is
■ They ■ are   . . . .
         ■ can be

Let's write

1   Oranges are...............................
2   Grass is...................................
3   Flowers can be........................
4   Hair can be.............................
5   Water......................................

6   Eyes..
7   The sky...................................
8   Apples.....................................
9   Trees.......................................

Let's talk

What's Tom doing?
- ■ Is he reading?
- ■ I think he's playing football.

What's . . . doing?

- ■ Is
  - ■ he
  - ■ she · · ·?

- ■ I think
  - ■ he's
  - ■ she's · · · ·

Let's write

1   Bill is...

2   John is...

3   Susan...

4   Tom...

5   Jill...

6   Christine..

7   Mary..

park   river   school   post office   station

Let's talk

Look at number one. Where is she going?
    I think she is going to the post office.

Look at number . . . .   Where ▪ is / ▪ are . . . going?

I think ▪ he / ▪ she / ▪ they ▪ is / ▪ are going to . . . .

Let's write

1   Number one: She is going to..

2   Number two:........................ is................. to................................

3   .... three: They are........................ to................................

4   .... four:........................ i................. to................................

5   .... five:..

6   .... six:..

Five children are in a cinema. Ann is sitting next to Bob. Bob is sitting next to a boy. Susan is sitting next to Mike and David. David is sitting next to a boy and a girl. Ann is sitting on the left.

Let's talk

I think David is sitting next to Ann. And you, Peter?
- ■ Yes, I think so, too.
- ■ No, I think David is sitting next to . . . .

I think . . . is sitting next to . . . . And you . . .?
- ■ Yes, I think so, too.
- ■ No, I think . . . is sitting next to . . . .

Let's write

1   Ann is sitting next to B..

2   Bob is sitting..

3   Susan is sitting...

4   David...

5   Mike..

29 twenty-nine

Let's draw and write

1 Draw a cat *under* the chair.

2 Draw a box *on* the table.

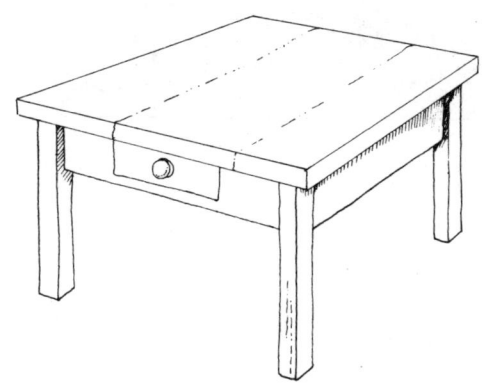

3 Write your name *on* this line:

4 Draw a girl *in* the circle.
5 Write 'girl' *under* the circle.

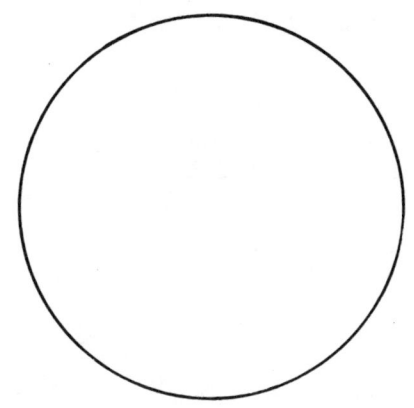

6 Draw three apples *in* the basket.

7 Draw a . . . . . *in* the box.
8 Draw a . . . . . *on* the box.
9 Write '. . . . . .' *under* the box.

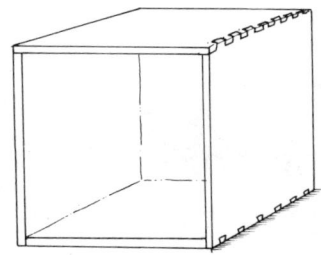

10 What's *behind* the tree?

11 What's *behind* the car?

in
on
next to
under
in front of
behind

Let's talk

Where's the box?

    Under a

    Next to . . . .

Where ■ 's / ■ are the . . .?

. . . ■ a / ■ the . . . .

Let's write

1   The bananas are ....

2   The basket is ....

3   The chocolate ....

4   The oranges ....

5   The ball ....

grass

flower

cloud

hill

bird

cart

tree

shoe

Let's talk

Where's number one in the picture?

 Just a minute. It's here. It's part of the grass.

Where's number . . . in the picture?

 Just a minute. It's here. It's ■ a . . . .
 ■ part of the . . . .

Let's write

1   One is part of the..

2   Two is p............... of the..

3   Three............... a..

4   F..

5   ....

6   ....

7   ....

8   ....

Let's talk

I can make 'dog'.   What can you make, Tom?
     I can make 'cat'.

I can make . . . .   What can you make, . . .?
     I can make . . . .

Let's write

I can make:...

....

Let's talk

Can you make a word and spell it?
- ■ Yes, number five is cow.
- ■ No, just a minute.

Can you make a word and spell it?
- ■ Yes, number . . . is . . . .
- ■ No, just a minute.

Let's write

one: ....

two: ....

three: ....

four: ....

five: ....

six: ....

seven: ....

eight: ....

nine: ....

ten: ....

eleven: ....

twelve: ....

thirteen: ....

fourteen: ....

fifteen: ....

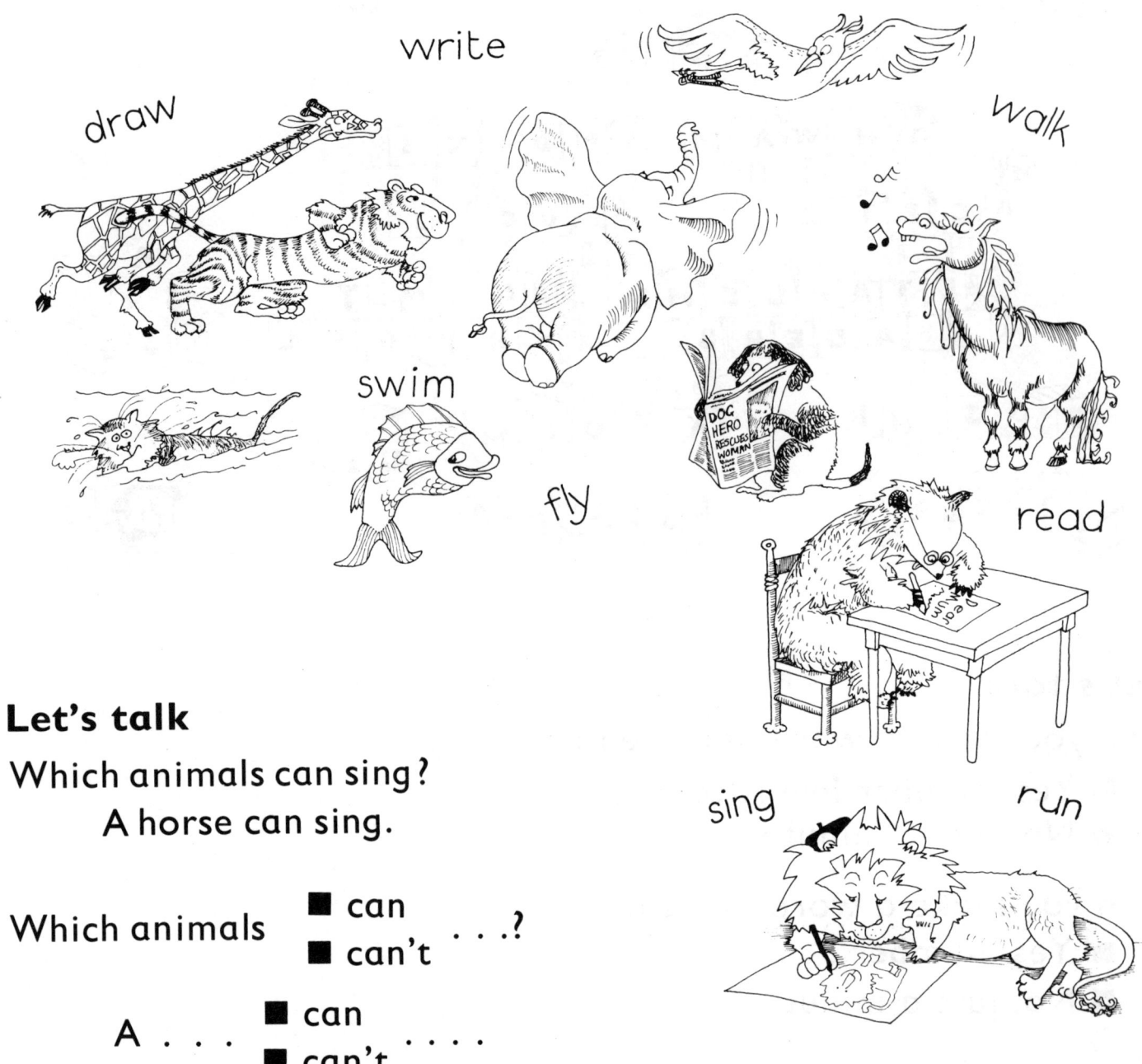

draw write walk swim fly read sing run

Let's talk

Which animals can sing?
    A horse can sing.

Which animals ■ can
              ■ can't   . . . ?

    A . . . ■ can
             ■ can't   . . . .

Let's write

1   A giraffe can......................................

2   A bear can't......................................

3   A tiger can......................................

7   A bird......................................

8   A......................................

9   A......................................

10   ....

4   A fish can't......................................

5   A lion c......................................

6   A dog c.........t......................................

Let's talk

I can see one coat. And you, Tom?
- ■ I can see one coat, too. And you Mary?
- ■ I can't. I can see two coats. And you, Lucy?

I can see . . . . And you, . . .?
- ■ I can see . . ., too. And you, . . .?
- ■ I can't. I can see . . . . And you, . . .?

Let's write

1	I can see...T-shirts.
2	I can see...socks.
3	I......................see...................................hats.
4	I...shoes.
5	I...pullovers.
6	....boots.
7	....coats.
8	....dress.

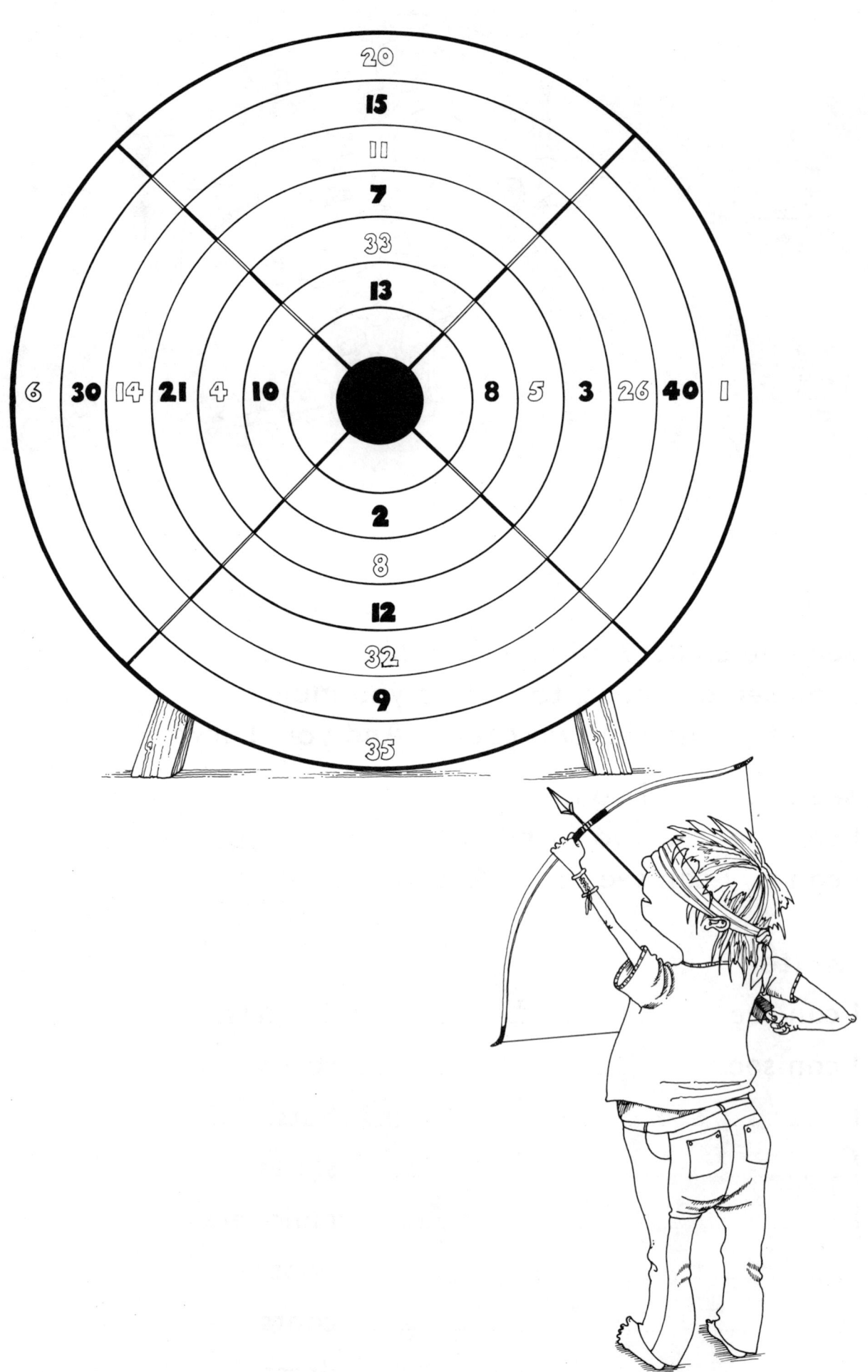

37 thirty-seven

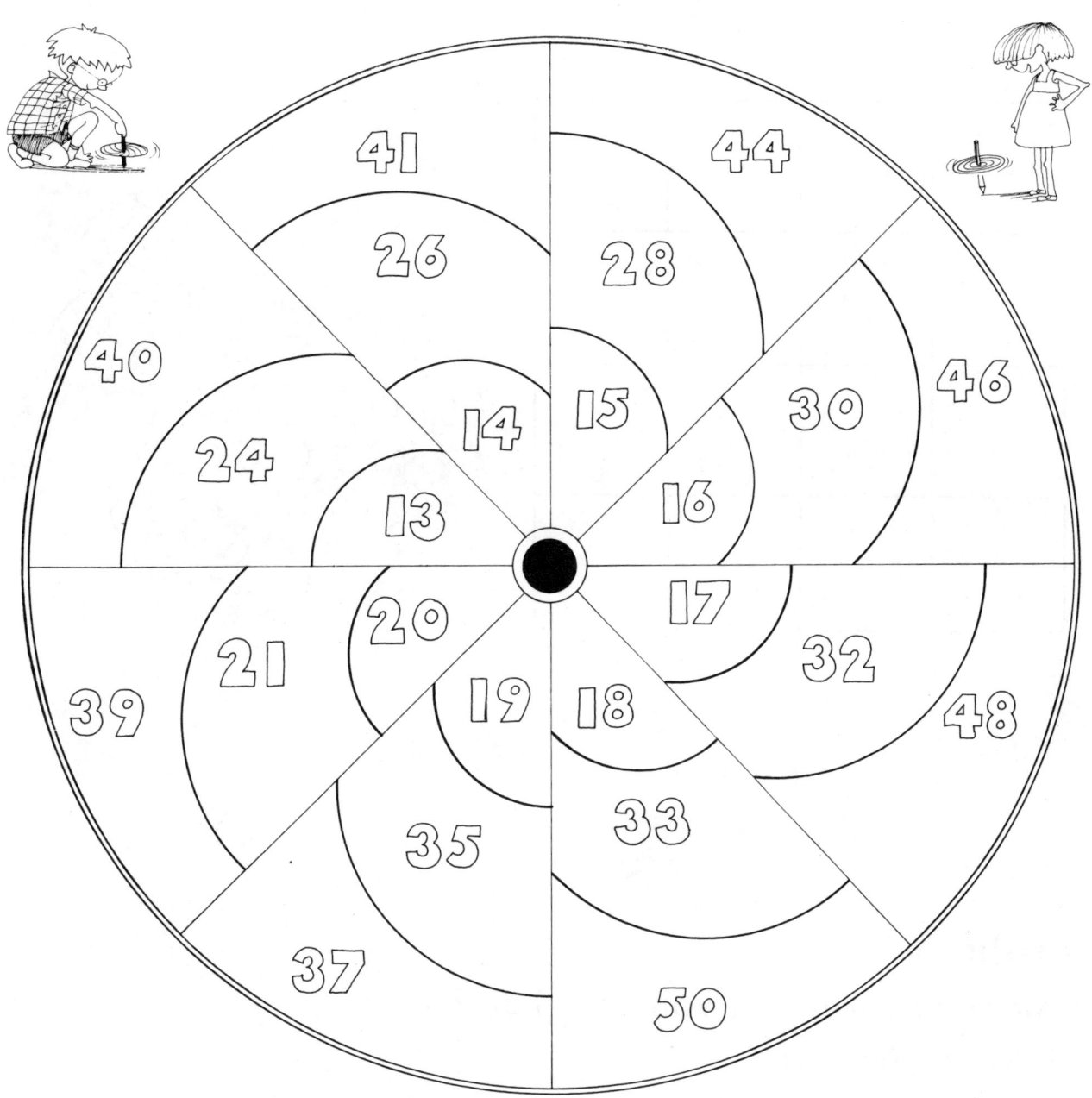

Let's talk

Number twenty on my top is green. What's number twenty on your top, Mary?

    It's . . . .

Number . . . on my top is . . . . What's number . . . on your top, . . .?

    It's . . . . What's number . . . on your top, . . .?

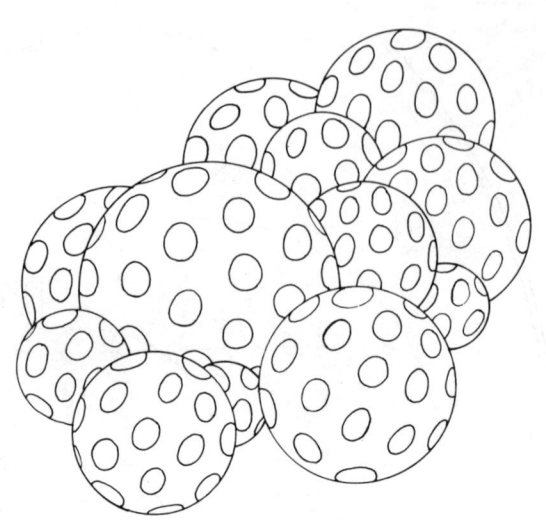

Let's talk

How many squares can you see, Tom?
> I don't know yet.

How many . . . can you see, . . .?
- ■ I can see . . . .
- ■ Just a minute. I can see . . . .
- ■ I don't know yet.

Let's write

How many squares can you see?

I..squares.

How many balls can you see?

I..balls.

Let's talk

What can you see beginning with 'p'?
    A pen, a pencil, and a pullover.

What can you see beginning with '. . .'?
- ■ . . ., . . ., . . . and . . . .
- ■ Just a minute. . . ., . . ., . . . and . . . .

Let's write

1   What can you see beginning with 'b'?

        b...

2   Beginning with 'c':...

3   Beginning with 'f':...

4   Beginning with 'g':...

5   's':...

6   'h':...

7   'p':...

8   'm':...

9   't':...

Let's talk

How old is the lion?

I think it's . . . . And you . . .?

How old is . . .?

■ I think
■ he's
■ she's . . . . And you, . . .?
■ it's

■ Just a minute. I think
■ he's . . . . And you, . . .?
■ she's

Let's write

1   Susan's mother is..

2   Susan's f.. is..........................

3   S....................'s s.. is..........................

4   S.......................... b.. is..........................

5   S.......................... g...

6   .... g...

Let's talk

Sally says 'Look, I'm wearing a white dress.' Which is Sally?
    I think she's G.

. . . says '. . .'. Which ■ is . . .?
    say   ■ are

            ■ he's . . . .
I think   ■ she's . . . .
            ■ they are . . . and . . . .

1   Susan and Bill say, 'Look, we're sitting on big chairs.'
2   Janet and David say, 'We can ride horses.'
3   Tom and Ann say, 'Look, we're sitting on small chairs.'
4   Peter says, 'I can ride a bike.'
5   Sally says, 'Look, I'm reading an English book.'
6   Kate says, 'Look, I'm writing in English.'

Let's write: can, I'm or are

1   *Susan and Bill:* Look, we........................sitting on big chairs.
2   *Sally:* I........................read English books. Look, I........................
     reading a book.
3   *Peter:* I........................ride a bike.
4   *Janet:* I........................riding a horse.
5   *David:* I........................ride a horse, too.

bed · chair · books · cat · table · man · woman · ball
some flowers · dog · some apples · toys · boy · some milk · girl · toy car

Let's talk and draw

What can we put in the living-room?

    Let's draw a chair.

What can we put in the . . .?

    Let's draw   ■ a . . . .
                  ■ some . . .s.

What's in your kitchen?
    There's a fridge.

What's in your . . .?

    There   ■ 's a . . . .
             ■ are some . . . .

Let's write: there is   there are

1   In the kitchen there...

2   In the l.........................-r.........................there.........................

3   In the ....there.........................

4   In the...

Let's talk

Is the roof of house 'A' like the roof of house 'B'?
    I don't know yet.

■ Is
■ Are   the . . . of house . . . like the . . . of house . . . ?

        ■ Yes,   ■ it is.
                  ■ they are.

        ■ No,   ■ it isn't.
                  ■ they aren't.

        ■ I don't know yet.

Let's write

1   The door of house............... is like the d............... of house...................

2   The roof of.. like the...

3   The windows of... like the...

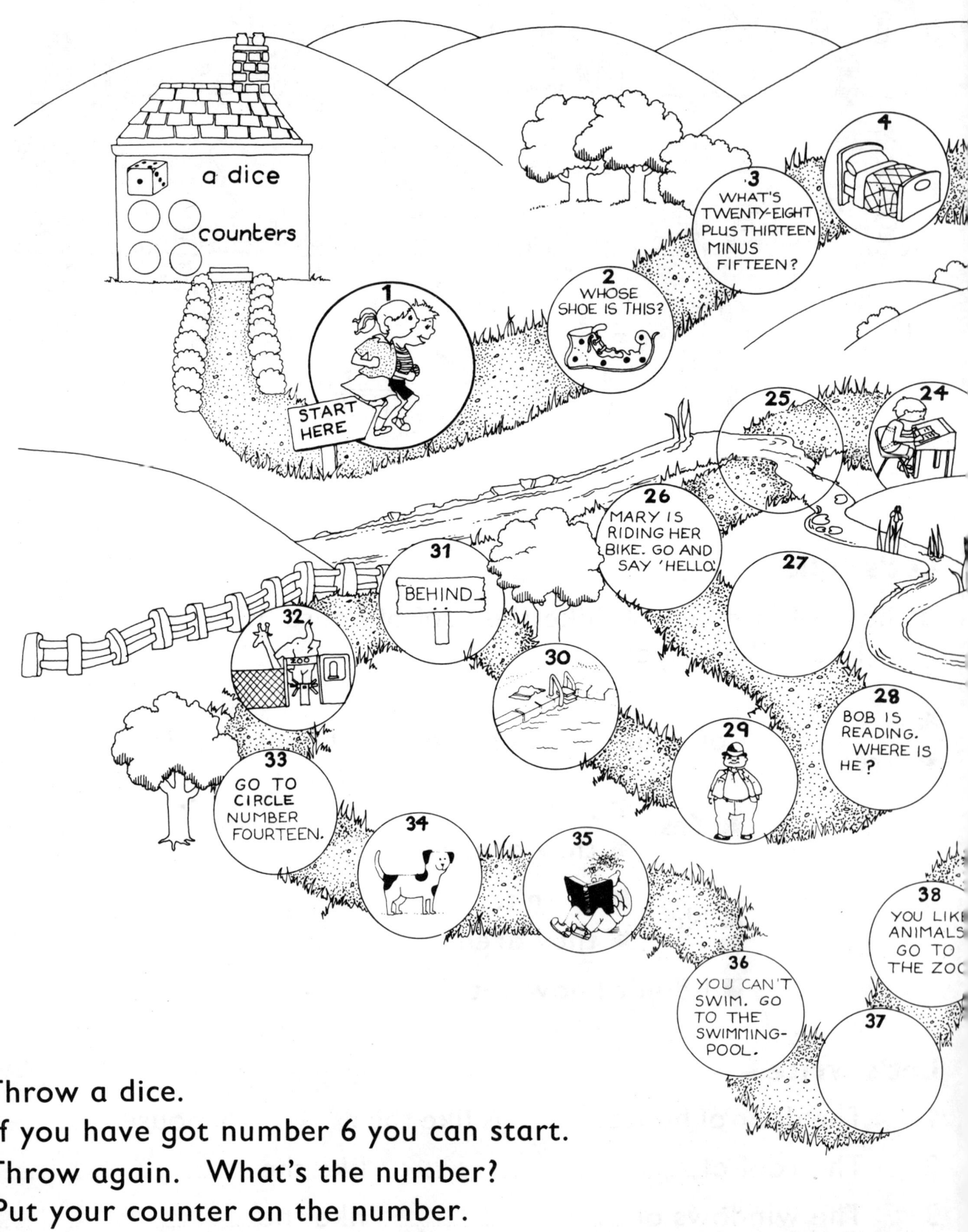

Throw a dice.
If you have got number 6 you can start.
Throw again.   What's the number?
Put your counter on the number.